NEW *ILLUSTRATED* ENCYCLOPEDIA OF GARDENING

UNABRIDGED

GARDENS AROUND THE WORLD

TERRACES, PATIOS, BALCONIES, WINDOW BOXES
GARDEN DÉCOR, PLANTING, AND POOLS

TEXT BY ELIZABETH SCHULER

WITH AN INTRODUCTION AND NOTES

BY PETER PESEL

 GREYSTONE PRESS · NEW YORK

Library of Congress Catalog Card Number: 64—20293

First Published in the United States of America by Harry N. Abrams, Incorporated, New York

All rights reserved. No part of the contents of this book may be reproduced

without written permission of the publishers

Greystone Edition designed by Harold Franklin

Published 1966 Greystone Press, New York

TABLE OF CONTENTS

INTRODUCTION

The owner of a garden will surely appreciate the American philosopher, Thoreau, who once remarked that he had travelled extensively — in Concord. And Concord, a sleepy little town, was anything but worldly. But a garden, skilfully planned — in Concord or anywhere else — brings much of the world to our door.

This can even be done successfully in a cottage garden: a little bit of Mexico with nasturtiums (not merely with cacti); North Africa with mignonette; Turkey and Persia with pansies and lilac; southern Siberia, China, and the Himalayas with larkspur; and Holland with tulips, thanks to a Dutchman named Busbeck, ambassador to the court of the Caliph, who fell in love with them and brought them back to Europe in 1561.

The tulip and the other flowers introduced by Busbeck were not the only plants that an inhabitant of the Old World brought home from abroad. Three thousand years before him, Hapshepsut, Queen of Egypt, equipped a whole expedition to collect trees from foreign parts, trees such as olibanum and date palms. Once she had these trophies in her garden, she ordered that the trees be surrounded by walls on which she had recorded pictorially the adventures and difficulties of transporting her treasures.

No one knows how the Garden of Eden looked. What was the hedge around the Garden like? In Genesis it merely says that it contained "every tree that is pleasant to the sight, and good for food". Mohammed promised that apart from two specimens of every fruit-bearing plant, and in addition to two ever-flowing streams, the faithful would enjoy the company of beautiful houris.

The gardens in which man tries to reproduce or to reconstruct his own conception of Paradise, can only attempt to be replicas of the original. What grows in Pompeii or the monastery of St. Gallen or the orangery at Versailles is possibly good to eat, but it hardly conveys the idea of Paradise, and in addition may become formidable problems in one's own garden. What path a branch is to take in the air, what shape a tree is to have, is decided by the shears and by the nature of whatever delicate or severe patterns happen to be in fashion, as well as by the tree itself.

In the seventeenth century, gardens were represented by bright stones; their feeling of life, by a host of fountains. Not only did nothing flower in them; nothing was grown any more. Man had finally tamed nature, imposing his order upon her ineluctably. Only the peasant and monastery gardens looked different. Yet, even in monasteries flowers were used only as medicinal herbs or as adornment for altars. Antirrhinums, pinks, hollyhocks, roses, and lilies, stocks and gillyflowers sufficed to recall that the world is more than an orderly combination of mathematics and morals.

One must not blame the Italians for not being as emphatic about flowers as the Dutch: after all, Eskimos wear brighter clothes than Bedouins. Where the sky itself dons overpowering colours every day, few long for a little patch of red or yellow. Nevertheless, Mijnheer Busbeck's was a marvellous achievement. Leyden, where he sowed the seeds, produced Asiatic blossoms. Imperial lilies and "Peruvian" scillas (there are no scillas in Peru; they actually come from Anatolia and Persia) suited the grey Renaissance which held Europe in thrall. From Leyden the narcissus conquered Europe; presumably it also came from Turkey. But anyone who thinks that the gardens were filled with flowers is mistaken. The gardens remained without blossoms. The blossoms covered the broad fields just like cabbages, or they were grown in pots — hundreds of them — placed in rows. For flowers to be allowed to grow in gardens is a comparatively recent privilege. Even the English gardens, which owe their origin to China, at best contained only flowering trees.

The owner of a garden today, even if it be only ten yards long and five yards wide, can profit from the ingenuity of aspiring gardeners and the natural resources of other lands thousands of miles away. Tazzetta narcissus came from Gibraltar, jonquils from Seville, the scented narcissus from Steiermark. A skilful gardener can record not only history but geology. Should a man with a green thumb manage to grow on his piece of land certain New Zealand plants, he will trace their relatives in Europe back to the Carboniferousera: ferns as tall as trees; evergreens with metallic shiny leaves; columbines with scarlet bills and their dark red sisters, the smaller parrot peas; and grey luxuriant climbing plants. Not far removed from these in the history of the earth are the acacias of Australia which are better known in Europe and far easier to grow.

In the European gardens of the Middle Ages gardening was a somewhat haphazard affair. A garden was merely a living room in the open air: a wall with a little gateway set in it. Behind it was a carefully tended lawn, a well, a tree, and stone benches. Admittedly people lived in this garden, ate, dallied, played, argued, and made music. They believed that a garden must have a tree for the sun to tinge red at morning and evening; there must be silence and room for gaiety; ideally there must be water.

The recipe for a "real" garden seems to be Chinese, Taoist, in fact (although it could just as well be Japanese or old Persian). The historians of religion can sing a doleful lay of how the expulsion from Paradise, the violent estrangement from life in the gardens, has affected the unadorned histories of earlier civilizations. Historical associations apart, before the blossoms come, the soil of a garden must be prepared with the aid of fertilizers, perhaps a compost heap, and a few earthworms in the loamy earth which does not as yet deserve the name of soil. And above all, we must know what we are going to grow. Some plants need acid, some need alkalis, some require other elements. Before we talk about shrubs and trees, we must dispense with generalizations, and first of all do some hard work with the spade. Otherwise we shall be left without either trees or shrubs.

There are people who start their garden by putting a fence round a piece of land, but the fence is not the most important thing in a garden: the less seen of a fence, the better. A garden must have many entrances and many paths must be allowed to lead to it.

And when will the garden really be a success! When a robin appropriates a favoured bush; when a family of squirrels steals nuts from the terrace and stuffs them in a hole in the tree; when a lizard suns itself on an artificially laid stone path; when a cheery warbler makes its perch above the garden. In short, when all of nature is in harmony and "at home," then your own labours will be rewarded and man's contriving and nature's own contribution will have been skilfully blended.

GERMANY
AND
AUSTRIA

The Drostes in Meersburg are lucky enough to possess an old, well tended vineyard as a garden, including an attractive cottage with peonies, roses, and stocks, and a royal shooting box transformed into an incomparable theatre. The Alps serve as a back drop, hundreds of sailing boats as props, and clouds, gulls and herons as actors. In addition to this, every year the sun and the rain produce a few vats of Burgundy and Traminer. But such luxury is by no means essential. For instance, asparagus are not to be despised. Goethe grew them with his own hands. He sent some to Frau von Stein, who naturally invited him to taste the results of his labours, ennobled by her culinary art — as the gardener had probably intended. (Asparagus can after all be considered "flowers" and they are well-suited to bachelor gardens.) With a bouquet of tulips which he had grown himself, he would not have had the same success. This example proves the value of a vegetable garden where plants and vegetables can be grown together and act as a flower garden also.

We can only guess whether Goethe appreciated stone dwarfs and plaster deer. Since he had sufficient imagination to people his world with figures of his own creation, he may well have been satisfied with unadorned, well-trimmed terraced lawns upon which to sit.

A recipe which, in addition to his succulent menus, enabled Prince Pückler to achieve lasting fame was the landscape garden with all manner of vistas through which one could wander at leisure along flowering paths and among shrubberies. The setting of the garden and the landscape behind, formed a single unit untrammelled by boundaries or fences. Using shrubs and trees wisely is a favourite trick of landscape gardeners when they wish to conceal something: the bathing pool and seating areas from the eyes of neighbours, the refuse corner from the notice of the visitor, the street from the owner who desires privacy. Usually the terrain is left as it is, steep or level, flat or undulating. Or the garden may be enhanced with elevations and valleys with the use of the spade, even if the elevation be only six feet high and the valley no larger than grandmother's kitchen rug.

A bright, luxuriant border of Phlox, Delphiniums, and Daisies provides a rustic atmosphere in this Alpine setting.

10

The Waterlily pool, with its reeds and sedge, teems with life — a variety of fish below and darting dragonflies above the water.

A house and garden in perfect harmony with the Alpine climate and landscape.

Far from the city, forest, meadow, and pool blend harmoniously.

A splendid example of the informal garden: not
too tidy; flowers wherever one looks; a rough
hewn wall, and steps leading up a grassy hillside.

Rhododendrons and Azaleas at the edge of a thicket.

A country garden near a brook. Phlox, Dahlias, and a mass of Nasturtiums blaze at the height of summer.

Sterling Silver

Souvenir de la Malmaison

Golden Shower: climbing rose

Sibelius

A superb bed of roses. In the foreground can be seen the giant blossoms of Gloria Dei.

17

A fresh spring border of glowing Tulips and dainty Forget-me-nots.

Climbing Roses are a beautiful covering for an unattractive wall.

A practical vegetable garden acquires a special beauty of its own with borders of colourful flowers.

wood glowing in full autumnal gold is the setting here for a thatched cottage surrounded by plane trees.

Tropical palms in an Alpine area are doubly dramatic, as in this display near Bad Reichenhall in Bavaria

FRANCE

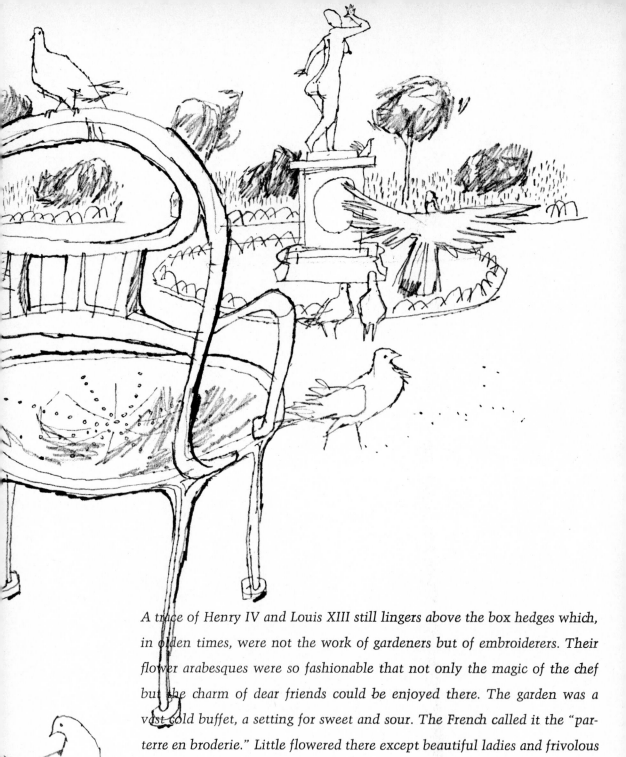

A trace of Henry IV and Louis XIII still lingers above the box hedges which, in olden times, were not the work of gardeners but of embroiderers. Their flower arabesques were so fashionable that not only the magic of the chef but the charm of dear friends could be enjoyed there. The garden was a vast cold buffet, a setting for sweet and sour. The French called it the "parterre en broderie." Little flowered there except beautiful ladies and frivolous chatter.

A slightly older renown clings to the rosebushes which stand before the grey houses, transforming them into a fairy tale setting.

Foremost among Botanical Gardens in Europe is France itself. People who do not know Brittany, to mention only one area, might think that "Botanical Garden" in France meant, inevitably, the Jardin des Plantes in Paris. Indeed on Sunday the whole of France is the setting of one vast "déjeuner sur l'herbe," while on weekdays nature appears in pots on the balcony, in front gardens, in roof gardens and in conversation.

Let us take a look at one of Colette's dream gardens: fennel and pansies; a pergola for climbing tulips and melons; daphne or Japanese calycanthus, both appreciated for their scent in winter; thousands of campanulas; pear, cherry and raspberry canes; blossoms as well as fruit, for both of these are well-loved. It is different in Japan where the blossoms are so revered that the fruit is forgotten. In the French garden then can be found all the charm of an English park, a historical formality, a certain delicacy, and the robust luxuriance of a hot summer.

As Lamartine has written, no owner of thousands of acres of land, or fields and streams in England and Scotland for instance, has more reverence for nature than the small gardener, when, on a Sunday, he can relax in his little garden under the few cherry trees he himself has planted; near the three beehives whose inmates buzz in the sunshine; near the flower beds which he himself has dug and which he will tend again tomorrow.

Rosa Centifolia

Baccarat

Lilies of the Valley

Cornflowers

26

An ingenious use of steps in the Begum's villa at Cannes.
From every crack summer flowers are in full bloom.

n this garden, everything is arran-
ed artistically to give height — the
teps, the columns, and even the
lender cypresses.

Hydrangeas and scarlet Geraniums provide a
refreshing splash of colour by a door leading to
the rocky coast.

The severity of this stone house is softened by the climbing Geraniums. Mimosa grows to a great height, while in the foreground there is a colourful display of Dwarf Cypresses, Petunias and Irises.

This French peasant cottage with its charming well, is alight with Geraniums, Daisies, Viburnum, and other flowering plants.

The sun and the sea are the key-notes of this Breton garden. The irregular pavement path provides the opportunity for growing some bright coloured rock plants.

A riot of colour greets the visitor to this house in Brittany. The roses have been carefully trained to climb as far as the roof.

It is easy to exploit such a beautiful wild setting;
one merely lets nature take its course.

A wild corner of a garden. Yellow and red roses grow in profusion contrasting with purple Buddleia and tall yellow candles of Verbascum.

A rich, lush garden on the Côte d'Azur. Note the gnarled boughs of the cork oaks. The varied greenery is in vivid contrast to the Scarlet Lychnis, Altheas and Campion.

ENGLAND

Hedges and stone walls are a protection from the wind which blows over the British Isles. The country seems to be covered with gardens, and in many places, to be one single garden. From the park at Blenheim whose lawns employ forty mowers daily — a constant work which can only be done at the cost of great labour — to the little wild flowering wilderness of a small cottage, everything can be found to delight the eye, including (surprisingly enough) romantic temples, urns, and statuary.

England is a good place for birds. Nowhere, with the possible exception of northern France, are there so many hedges and so many tracts of land undisturbed by humans, even when these regions, brackland or marsh, are tilled for produce.

English gardens, too, have room for human beings, for the lover of flowers. It is not for nothing that we are in the land in which the adopted Chinese garden became known as the English garden: what looks like decoration elsewhere is here luxuriant wilderness.

The English park, too, is actually Chinese in origin. (It is certainly not Elizabethan.) Perhaps that is why, in England, a garden represents neither a defeat of nature nor a blind obedience to her laws.

In no place in the world do Rhododendrons grow
more luxuriously than in England. Here you see
a 20 foot high hedge in which all possible shades
of this delightful flowering bush can be admired.

A romantic corner of the garden by a pond,
where the flowers are permitted to bloom
in their wild state.

This velvety lawn is a characteristic feature of English landscape gardening.

This garden is a knowing and tasteful example of the combining of nature and art: Rhododendrons, Azaleas, and wide green lawns are enhanced by fountains and charming stone cherubs.

One of those luxuriant borders and irregular pavements which are so typical of the English garden.

Lilac in full bloom

Hybrid Rhododendrons

Polyanthus and Moss Roses

Irises

A generously planned garden. In the foreground a glorious floral border of Lavender, Phlox, and Tiger Lilies. Behind, a pergola with Polygonum and climbing Roses.

Terraced rockeries, flower beds and wall plants
lead the eye naturally to the top of the wall and
to the tall Rose bushes.

...refully tended lawns,
...ergola with climbing
...ses, beds of Roses and
...vias give this English
...den its distinction.

Waterlilies gleam in the moat, and over the ancient walls Ivy, Virginia Creeper and Roses climb.
Flowering shrubs and clumps of flowers add ef-
fectively to the bank.

Rosebushes and tree Roses provide notes of pleasant variety to the long rows of suburban houses.

HOLLAND

Holland is one huge garden. It could be said that it is a commercial garden, but that would perhaps be only a half-truth. The commercial garden smacks too much of truck-gardens. In any case, who will take issue with the Dutch because the canals of this great garden are not, like those in India, provided with useless waterfalls, but instead carry ships full of gleaming red round cheeses, barges full of mysterious bulbs, passengers, and shrubs.

For 400 years this land has provided the gardens of Europe with flowers, and their perfume even extends to the schools of painting. Prior to this, grass and weeds were all that the human figures on the canvases could set their feet upon. The tulip was only a beginning and both Mijnheer Busbeck and his tulips found a number of successors to follow their example. We had to learn to see with Dutch eyes, so that we could begin to have a gardener's eye for other wild flowers. One of these flowers, the auricula or primrose, was first developed in all its splendour in Holland. The glistening black of the Dutch soil also shows where it was sown with bulbs, how much green and soft gleaming beauty it can produce, bear and nourish.

·In the old days the Dutch took their bulbs and seeds as seriously as other people took bars of gold. They gave a fortune for a handful of flowers. They even speculated with flowers. Today, thousands of bulbs are no longer worth a fortune. The financial tribute which we pay the land of flowers for the splendour of our spring and summer gardens, for the colours which lighten a greying autumn, is now less than our tribute of appreciation.

*Vari-coloured Phlox in full bloom against
the contrasting colour and shape of blue
Delphiniums and white Madonna Lilies.*

52

One glorious section of a beautifully laid out garden. A tasteful blending of well-tended lawns, a bright-coloured floral border, and rich green ornamental shrubs.

With great artistry all the flowers in this border are arranged according to their colours and shapes: the light and dark violet Veronica with the scarlet Lupins and the Catch-fly; yellow Yarrow and orange Bignonias or Trumpet Flowers; and behind them, dark blue Delphiniums and the purple bells of the Heuchera.

e landscape garden with its dwarf ergreens displays its bright spring ours. How beautifully the red ntrasts with the grey rock, and : blue Grape Hyacinths with the l-blown Tulips, Narcissi, wall-wers, Pansies and Hyacinths in ; gay setting.

Amaryllis

Narcissus and Pheasant's Eyes

Hyacinths

Tulips

55

Various types of prunus are valuable additions
to these gardens. In the foreground is a hybrid
malus floribunda, highly decorative with its
double pale pink blossoms.

A wonderful example of a well-planned gard.
that achieves harmony with contrasting colou
and a variety of shapes and heights.

This shady fishpond lies in front of a wood of
majestic evergreens ranging from blue to green.
Among them, are growing tall pink Foxgloves.

SCANDINAVIA

The Swedish peasant houses are like huge dark-red flowers with white borders. As a result the gardens in the cities must always be decorated with red tiles to appeal to the eye of the beholder. In Denmark, the houses are black and white. Danish modesty and the climate of Denmark forbid the exotic. Even the fences seem to have grown there naturally. They are coarsely made of finger-thick upright stakes of peeled pine or corrugated iron, and serve as protection against the sea wind and the eyes of neighbours. Climbing roses usually grow on both sides, or between the stakes. Sometimes the fence is purely symbolic, a low row of drift blocks and pebbles from which blossoms sprout in the spring as though the very stones had flowered. In Denmark, even in the hottest summers, the lawns are a brilliant green. The flowers have something of the Arctic spring in their colours, except that they look more domesticated than their wild sisters.

Denmark probably possesses the strangest garden in the world, just as Rio has the most spectacular, and Ceylon the most beautiful. It is at Odense. The Danes call it the fairy garden, Eventyrhaven. Not far away is the house where Hans Christian Andersen was born.

Buddleia

Laburnum

Moss Rose

This pool garden is a playground for adults and children alike. The garden bench is conveniently placed for watching the pleasant scene.

A springtime idyll composed of Polyanthus and Forget-me-nots.

A formal carpet of Tulips and Grape Hyacinths stretches beneath tall trees.

Huge scarlet Poppies give a dramatic splash of needed colour to the sun-parched greenery and a contrast to the wide blue sea.

In its colour and form this garden an exquisite composition: Clema Oleander, and Roses; a sophistica Lily pool in which goldfish swim.

Serenity is the keynote of this gentle landscaping. Among the Laburnum, Rhododendrons, and Peonies, a rustic birdhouse and birdbath add a pleasant decorative highlight.

A tidy, colourful flower bed and well-tended lawn complement the attractive house. A white sundial adds a nice touch of originality.

SWITZERLAND

In Swiss gardens it is always Sunday. They are incredibly tidy and they are nearly always in flower. When they are not actually in full bloom, everything is waiting for the next crop. This tidiness holds good for the very first peasant gardens the traveller sees as soon as he has crossed the frontier. They are no larger than elsewhere, but even when a fence is rusty, it is quite a different kind of rust from that to be found in Austria or Poland (where, incidentally, there are also charming peasant gardens). In Switzerland the rust seems to have been cleaned away as though someone had spent an hour or so rubbing it.

When the Swiss move into the city, they take their country garden with them. On the way it loses its fence, and is now surrounded by a carpet of mown grass which looks so immaculate that it appears to have been rolled out directly on the soil. Behind this green foreground, the old garden remains, full of colour and the hum of bees — a garland of welcome round each house, round each district. No flowers are ever picked, it would seem. There are beautiful gardens in Switzerland. Their creators are as able as they are modest. Here nature, the "wild one," will not be imitated, and the cleverest gardeners are content to let mountain and lake play the part of a background, and, according to the season, to allow the tints to change faster than autumn leaf. To produce this setting it needs only a surrounding wall, a cluster of trees, a wooden summer house, a few bushes, and plenty of lawns. The moment will come when the sausages will be left to burn on the grill because the owner falls beneath the spell of this enchanted landscape.

Where there is no lake in the vicinity — and this can happen even in Switzerland — creative gardeners will often build a pond and plant a few old trees on its bank. This is usually done so skilfully that with a little luck, wild duck will settle there and rear their young.

s original garden composition
bines the artistry of a Spanish
lattice with a picturesque old
wheel and a well.

The outstanding feature of this garden is a superb
Camellia which beams its radiance on the entire
area.

An irregularly-paved walk leads through a wrought iron gate to a severe yet attractive garden of tree Roses and varied evergreens.

The Tessin is full of surprises. Mountains, lakes, and tropical date palms, an old mill wheel and feathery pampas grass make an unexpectedly Swiss garden.

*A skilful and tasteful use of climbing Roses en-
riches a home and garden by the lakeside.*

ITALY

Since the days of Pliny, nature and art have vied with each other in the Italian garden: plants and marble, trees and statues. Fountains and the skilful use of running water have made it unique. The contrast between light and shade, cypresses and sunshine serves as a background. Often the sun wins the contest and the plants lose; the stone weathers, and the fountains dry up.

When the West first rediscovered the world of plants and created the science of botany, it was at Salerno in Italy. Salerno at the time was occupied by the Arabs. Before that time there was no mention of herb women for there was no need to turn their handiwork into a science: it was taken for granted that they knew where the healing plants grew and which of them was beneficial to man.

Tasso, grieving for the hard-hearted Lucrezia Bendidio, bids the wind bear away his sighs. He remembers that the wind renders the same services to the sweet-scented flowers of the oleander and the myrtle. The fact that he summarily names the laurel and the myrtle as vital for girls in search of husbands reveals the role that the Italian flora played in those days: it was an arsenal of requisites.

Italian gardens, as Boccaccio proved, were really only intended to give aesthetic pleasure. The Italians enjoy colours, scent and shady arbors. Wells and concealed watercourses are praised. All manner of "harmless animals" are admired and garlands are woven out of various materials as they grow within reach on the paths. Today sunbathing and afternoon tea are the latest innovations. But in the setting for these enjoyments, no change can be perceived. There is still a purely classical aura, a sense of history, surrounding these gardens.

A beautiful formal garden near Florence with everything severe and controlled: the box hedges, the jardinières, and the pool with its Waterlilies and Irises.

A broad terrace, flanked with majestic trees, is typically Italian in its use of pots and jardinières of flowers.

Camellia

Oleander

Cactus in bloom

A breathtaking display of Rhododendrons and Azaleas. At the end of the path lies the purple blue of Lake Como.

Cypresses loom decoratively against the sky and at the same time give shelter from the wind which blows from the mountains. The pots have been planted with Orange and Lemon trees.

Along these weathered terrace steps grows a combination of Petunias, Geraniums, Zinnias, and cacti of several types, with handsome clay jardinières interspersed.

In this lush southern setting, Bougainvillea grows around the
entrance and the arch, and ceramics make a tasteful decoration.

SPAIN

The gardens of modern Spain are predominantly green. This colour means
a great deal in a brown, parched land. But in the former Omayyid kingdom,
since the first Emir, Abd Er Rahman, waterfalls from the lily ponds, bright
blue fields of iris, white lilies, narcissus, pomegranates, and date palms have
flourished. Abd Er Rahman did not have to read Pliny to know that the
best landscape gardeners were to be found in Syria; he himself came from
Damascus. His ambassadors were sent to Turkestan and to India in search
of new plants and rare seeds. Green was not enough even though it was
the colour of the turban that distinguished the nephew of the Prophet from
the host of Believers. In the 8th century when Boniface was teaching the

Germans to chant in the monastery of Fulda, the Moslem Emirs of Cordova would give two loaves of bread for a single narcissus for while bread stilled the hunger of the body, a blossom stilled the hunger of the soul.

From Christian Byzantium ambassadors came to see what had happened to the most beautiful blossoms of Persia and India in the hands of rulers who were famous for their love of flowers and estates. It was told that the last Omayyid, Caliph Mutamid, created a sea of blossoms for his wife, Rumaykiija, a famous poetess, who longed to see the snow. When she begged to be allowed to journey to the snow or to have the snow brought to Cordova, the Caliph promised her the second. Came the next winter, and the hills round Cordova bloomed white one morning with a thousand flowering almond trees.

The Gul-i-Mazar, the "flower of the graves," still blooms where the Arab princes of Granada were laid to rest, and the azure blue of this iris is still today one of the favourite colours of Spain. The white iris of the Moorish cemeteries has become the flower of the Madonna, and the lily of the Mohammedan women's tombs became the escutcheon of the knightly order of our Lady and the emblem of Andalusia. But the powerful influence of the Indian garden copied in Spain is shown also for, as Buddha holds a lotus blossom, so does the Virgin depicted by the painters of Christian Spain hold a water lily.

the patio, a flowerless garden,
om which one may enjoy the
erra, shimmering in the haze.

A superb show of climbing Roses
with the avantage of summer-long
bloom.

A golden Spanish courtyard wit[h]
view of the sea. Stones in the n[atu]-
ral setting have been used as d[eco]-
ration. Among them grow Mes[em]-
bryanthemum or Fig-marigolds, [&]
Oenothera or Evening Primroses.

Among the common plants such as Pansies and
Geraniums, palm trees and paintings on the
wall give a particular flavour to this garden.

Here again is typical warm climate vegetation. A huge agave in the foreground furnishes a dramatic highlight.

Irregular stepping stones in an artificial pool, water plants, shrubs, and tall trees. An example of good "natural" flowering.

The coolness and privacy of a Spanish courtyard are here duplicated with climbing blossoms, tall trees, and a wall bordering an irregular stone walk leading to a wrought iron gate.

*xpansive garden of the typical
ern type with box hedges, palms,
agaves, and a host of pots and
ary to give colour to the scene.*

In the warm climate near the coast,
cacti, palms, and other exotic plants
thrive, enriching the scenery with
their fantastic shapes.

A southern garden with Eucalyptus trees and
Oleanders. Cannas stand dramatically in huge
earthenware pots.

GREECE

Acacia blossoms against the sky, robbing it of little of its colour because it is too pale. Wisteria makes the same effort and droops no longer when the sun begins to set. This is good, for otherwise the acacias and the wisteria would appear to be the same colour. And colour is rare in Greece. The spring cannot be delayed here and the places where the goats and the long forgotten statesmen made the paths on the bare mountain slopes, must take on the appropriate colours. One man, who must have known, affirmed that the ancient Greeks were no gardeners.

Grace grows wild in this country. It is there, and one hardly needs to plant it. The pathetic shaggy gardens have as much grace as a girl who appears out of a crumbling hovel, enchanting the fortunate traveller who sees her, without artifice and without make-up.

Roses and pomegranates are sometimes protected here with fences, but the owner rarely takes the fences seriously. He lets them decay so that the roses clamber over them in profusion and the pomegranates blossom within reach.

This is the nature of the country. Even the ruins of Mycenae have no garden, but the marjoram turns the wilderness into a sea of blossom, and the verbascum thrives around Agamemnon's grave.

If we could return to the groves of Academe, what would we find remaining of their knowledge and their self-assurance? Chatter blown away by the wind. Long-winded speeches caught in the rustling leaves of the ilex. Possibly in such a setting some learned man may have thought that people should not casually break off pomegranate blossoms in this land. For it could always happen that someone might steal from the tree which had borne the golden apples of the Hesperides. In Greek gardens it would be quite possible. Ancient philologists nurse such thoughts, particularly about midday when the eyes smart in the pitiless sunshine, and Pan can steal unnoticed from the obscurity of a distant wood.

*A garden in classic style with tall
cypresses, topiary, an artificial pond,
and a bed of Petunias and Zinnias.*

A typical peasant house in the lonely countryside. Note the profusion of flowers in the pots and pans.

Pines, luxuriant summer flowers, and green lawns flank a handsome path of wide-set flagstones leading to the water's edge.

A most interesting mosaic is crea with sculptured house walls, geor tric fence designs and the carefu laid paving stones in an echoing p tern. Red geraniums bring a softn and gaiety to the rectilinear form

BULGARIA

The side garden of the house shown
in the previous page. Here the pines,
twisted by the sea wind, provide
shade from the brilliant sun as well
as natural individual designs.

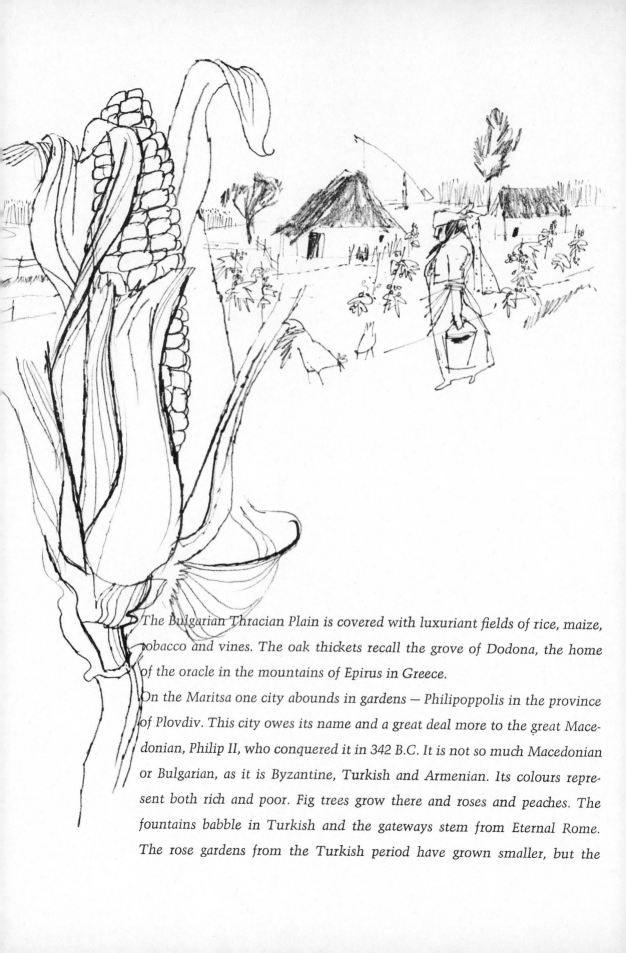

The Bulgarian Thracian Plain is covered with luxuriant fields of rice, maize, tobacco and vines. The oak thickets recall the grove of Dodona, the home of the oracle in the mountains of Epirus in Greece.

On the Maritsa one city abounds in gardens — Philipoppolis in the province of Plovdiv. This city owes its name and a great deal more to the great Macedonian, Philip II, who conquered it in 342 B.C. It is not so much Macedonian or Bulgarian, as it is Byzantine, Turkish and Armenian. Its colours represent both rich and poor. Fig trees grow there and roses and peaches. The fountains babble in Turkish and the gateways stem from Eternal Rome. The rose gardens from the Turkish period have grown smaller, but the roses are still there in plenty. The poplars stand like huge fans in the hot blue air and cast their shadows on bazaar and coffee house.

The gardens are a riotous wilderness. Their luxuriance is only curbed in front of the cool peristyles or courts and the wooden and stone columns of the loggias. Their scent is wafted across these frontiers and at night the songs of the bulbul and other birds are heard.

Does the old God of the gardens and the vineyards, whom the Thracians called Hero, still reside there? In the old days he was their favourite deity. He is portrayed as a Knight and the irises spring from the ground beneath the hooves of his horse. Wherever he looks the air is suddenly alive with bird song. His raiment smells like honey and is a magnet for the early spring bees. His sword has long since grown rusty for he was the first warrior to discover the power of gentleness. With a last burst of martial laughter, he enjoyed the obedience of the wild creatures that surrounded him and cleaved a passage for him whenever he appeared. The brambles parted and all the leaves and blossoms turned towards him. The animals accompanied him and wherever his passage led the desert disappeared, giving place to a row of young peach trees beneath which lilies grew.

*row of poplars and a tall hedge of
climbing Roses disguise a functional
wire fence.*

A cottage garden features masses of Mrs. Simpkins Pinks.

One of the huge rose fields outside Sofia. The delicate scent is incomparable.

Floribunda Roses.

The Oriental Rose from which attar of roses is made.

Two varieties of climbing Rose decorate the entrance to a walled garden.

Roses, the true emblem of Bulgaria are used here to adorn a house with velvety colour. A rich green vine trained over the pergola.

116

A colourful and extensive rock garden with Poppies, Armeria, and Daisies.

TURKEY

The fairy tale of Roses Bey, who never looked at a woman but travelled far and wide in search of unknown roses of which he had heard, appears to be a parable of the exaggerated oriental love of flowers. But since Roses Bey was one of the heroes whose story was told at night by the caravan watchmen, a vestige of him must remain hidden in the simplest Turk.

The land of the Thousand and One Nights still survives in the gardens of Turkey and in the voluptuous splendours of a Turkish garden party. There are, of course, no more viziers or sultans, but there are still tulips and perhaps tulip feasts at which the blossoms are adorned with candles, canaries in fragile cages, gay little lanterns, and glass balls filled with coloured water.

Flowers are also used in their thousands to drape the garden buildings and arches.

In the old days, Turkish conquerors set forth from Asia Minor to enslave the whole of Europe. An army of Janissaries, Turkish soldiers, helped them to victory. The Turks today have at their disposal a world wide organization which enables them to be on the spot to renew this victory at any given moment: Interflora. The only international body which everyone accepts willingly, Interflora's finances are reckoned not in marks, dollars, or roubles, but in flowers. It is not used nearly enough.

This house and garden could on
be found in Turkey Blazing r
Parrot Tulips and mauve Silene gro
in great profusion.

Massed Hydrangeas in a range of colours give
an opulent effect to this border.

Formal in pattern and delicate in design, the curves of this garden are highlighted with plantings of Daisies, Tulips, and Pansies.

Flowering fruit trees in an orchard rise from a carpet of Buttercups.

In this garden, feathery evergreens, softly draping vines, and colourful blooms make a frame
for the blue Bosporus.

In a small garden, a profusion of blooms.

AMERICA

Along the edge of a pool wanders a
path edged with Tulips, Phlox, and
Aubretia, also known as Purple Rock-
cress.

One might imagine that all the gardens in the world had been conceived in America, for anything that exists anywhere else can also be found here: the Renaissance garden, the Spanish (with tiles brought piece by piece from overseas), the French baroque garden, the English, and the Japanese. Only when one looks closer does one perceive that everything is a little more luxuriant than the original, perhaps a little more perfect. Nature helps by providing an almost complete pattern of all the climatic zones of the world. Original gardens on the American continent are to be found only in the soil of the ancient cultures of Mexico, Peru or Chile. In the earliest Aztec monastery gardens, plants and men were assembled according to the utterances of the astrologers. Before a patient was given an herb he was also asked his place of birth. Then, whenever possible, he was given herbs which were native to the place of his growing up.

The American garden is an enterprising triumph over the hazards of transplanting foreign-bred seedlings, a perfecting of techniques initiated in Europe. It is an intoxicating exotic cocktail of shapes, colours, and scents. As a background there are two oceans, mountains with giant unscaled peaks, deserts, and marshy tropical jungle.

A certain American book on gardening contains the observation that it is not difficult to make a good garden with an unlimited supply of money, soil and time, but emphasizes that it is quite possible for anybody, to make a charming garden without any of these three. There follows an example of how to make it, and it is a feast for the eyes and a joy to the hand. Though small, it included lawns, flowering shrubs, an herb garden, a place to dry the laundry, a verandah with tree stumps, vegetable beds, and a place for men and animals.

ttle patio is given the feeling of
mple garden with a small pool
ounded by Petunias, Daisies, Ge-
ums in pots, and greenery.

*A most inviting belvedere, where one can rest
amidst scented Heliotrope, and Snapdragons and
Astilbe.*

s garden dis-
s Almond trees
Copper Bee-
as well as a
zed border of
e Tulips to set
he blazing reds
pinks.

Cannas ranging from deep red,
through orange to the tenderest yellow enrich this Mexican garden.
Red and white Geraniums bloom
thickly in the background.

Along a bright white-painted fence, red Roses climb, accentuated by a border of pale mauve Irises alongside the walk.

This white columned "temple" was erected in honour of a rosebush. On either side of it, tall Hollyhocks, white, pink, red, and salmon-coloured against the blue of Campanulas and Cornflowers, and the white of Daisies.

136

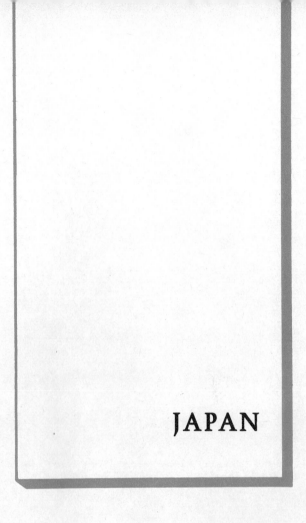

JAPAN

*A glory of spring-
time blooms from
Tulips, to Azaleas,
to Dogwood and
Cherry blossoms.*

It has been written — as we can read in Okakura — that peonies must be watered by a beautiful well-dressed girl, and a winter plum, by a slim, pale monk. But neither of these have any place in the Japanese garden.

The Japanese garden is a serious, philosophical landscape. The stones of the rockery recall the mountains, where lie the lonely Zen monasteries. The host of different mosses which spread over the stone are the soft element that tempers the harshness and mutes the noises of the busy town, beyond the bamboo hedges.

The Japanese garden was not always so green, grey, and unpretentious (apart from the tree which stands in the west so that the sun can set behind *it and turn it red for a short while). Eight hundred years ago, before the samurai began to rule, it was a riot of plum and cherry blossoms. Its pools were animated playgrounds for beautiful Chinese junks, and not the "motionless mirror of the eternal." Today only stones lie in them. Little stones which protrude just far enough out of the water to remind tea drinkers how far the circles can spread, how the small can be turned into the large. Anyone with a sterner sense renounces the grace of nature, lays the stones in carefully raked waves in the white sand, and banishes all plants from the garden until only a single blossom remains in the tokonoma, the alcove of the teahouse, and the silence is undisturbed. The Japanese garden seems made for the teahouse. In a square or round stone jar the rain water is collected in a bamboo ladle. Small stone lanterns light the vessels and the garden by night, and the stepping stones which lead through the garden to the teahouse demand a leisurely gait. The visitor to the teahouse leaves the garden behind him so that it merely prepares but does not intrude on him. When the gardener observes the rules of the Zen school, he never sweeps the garden because it would leave behind traces of disturbance. So the leaves lie there like souls in meditation.*

Anyone who wishes to be reminded of cherry blossoms must go elsewhere, perhaps to a Shinto temple.

But in these green, grey gardens there is plenty to admire, starting with the fences. What cannot be made out of bamboo and wood? Their form is legion — vertical, horizontal, diagonal, compressed or woven bamboo, whole or split stems of the greatest severity. So much for the outside. Within one finds the "short hedge" which lengthens the house walls like blinkers and bars a view into rice paper doors. The small low bridges with tall arches are so enchanting, that the eye, accustomed to reinforced concrete spans, is surprised and gratified.

e Japanese love to divide their
dens by gates and sometimes by
dges. Here a graceful gateway with
ors of woven bamboo is enhanced
a huge stone lantern.

Many different varieties of green plant, shrub,
and tree surround a path of natural rocks and
one of raked gravel. In the foreground, along the
terrace edge, a bright spark of flower bed.

A small area so beautifully landscaped that it gives the impression of a serene and spacious garden — a particular talent of the Japanese.

A European type garden, Japanese only in its understatement and in its insistence on water.

fully placed natural rock
es small cascades of the water
falls into the pond. Along
banks reeds and evergreen
ts droop gracefully over the
er.

Here again, the Japanese gardener displays a
careful selective planting, a sparing use of colour,
a lucid design.

The beautiful door and the fence are both of woven bamboo. Large rounded paving stones lead to the door, and in the background gleam gold-coloured blossoms of the Ranunculus.

Around a quiet pool, sand and gravel, artfully placed flat stones and natural rock, are softened with grasses, dwarf sycamore, evergreens and, here and there, flowering Azalea.

Amidst the ferns and soft mosses in this garden, the brook flows gently. The blue porcelain garden seats and table bring colour to a flowerless setting. The stone lanterns and the well are for use as well as beauty.

Delicacy and balance characterize this garden
with its slender birches, graceful low flowerbeds
and the gleam of a pool to one side.

Interesting use is made of white stones and
natural rock in this pool to make it fit more
easily into its setting. In the background there
are flower beds and Roses in bloom.

Double Japanese Prunus

Lotus — Waterlilies

Camellia Japonica

Chrysanthemum

Peonia albiflora: Kasha-no-mai
Japanese Peonies

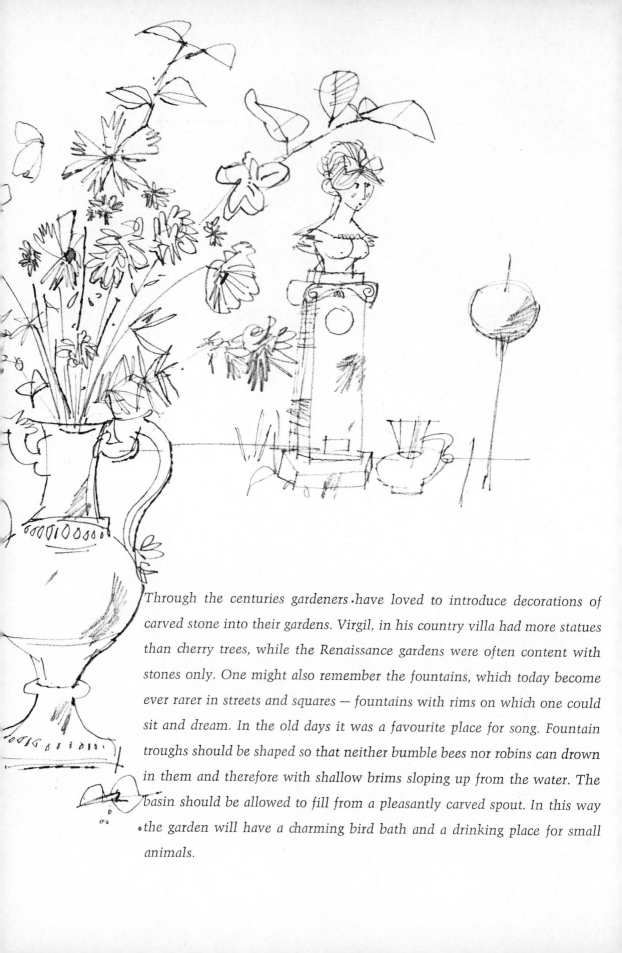

Through the centuries gardeners have loved to introduce decorations of carved stone into their gardens. Virgil, in his country villa had more statues than cherry trees, while the Renaissance gardens were often content with stones only. One might also remember the fountains, which today become ever rarer in streets and squares — fountains with rims on which one could sit and dream. In the old days it was a favourite place for song. Fountain troughs should be shaped so that neither bumble bees nor robins can drown in them and therefore with shallow brims sloping up from the water. The basin should be allowed to fill from a pleasantly carved spout. In this way the garden will have a charming bird bath and a drinking place for small animals.

GARDEN DECORATION

The gardener has a certain advantage over the goldsmith. He simply lays his plans and waits until the jewels appear of their own accord. The settings are the birdhouses for colourful songbirds or quiet visitors. A true garden lures such creatures. Such a garden also has a sun-kissed stone on which an emerald green lizard can sun itself. No large glass windows reflecting the sky will be found in such a garden. When glass walls are used, the prudent gardener will protect them with slatted curtains or trellis work. (Transparent glass walls in loggias and summer houses too often lure small birds to their deaths.)

In some old gardens there are tall, sturdy trees from whose branches two ropes can dangle. The two branches can hold a swing and here a boy or girl can try to emulate the Peacock or the Swallowtail butterfly. A special enchantment lives in the garden enhanced by tasteful decoration.

A tree trunk sawn in half makes a garden bench that can fit unobtrusively into natural surroundings.

A scarlet water wheel brings a dash of colour to the green of Eucalyptus trees, Banana palms, and grass.

An open hearth has been built at the end of a low wall, in careful harmony with its flowering neighbourhood.

Smooth concrete walls at different levels here provide a clean line against which the soft draping of plants into the water, and of growing water grasses show delicately.

A stone well provides both cool water and a handsome decoration.

Flower boxes have been built directly into the wall, breaking up an unrelieved expanse with bright patches of growing colour.

Hand-hewn stones surround this pool, giving an interesting texture to an otherwise undecorative form. A lush border of flowers and greenery provides a background against which to view the sculptured figure mounted in the centre of the pool.

A pergola gives an opportunity for overhead
flowering and a spot of inviting shade.

A piece of statuary adds importance to a small
pool of simple design.

A wheelbarrow filled to overflowing with growing flowers.

Where a tree stump cannot be removed, it can be used as a support for climbing flowering plants.

The level rock garden needs added interest: a Japanese lantern, different sizes of stone jars, a birdhouse, as here, or other selected ornaments.

Wrought iron is used in a delicate tracery against the white walls of this house in a lantern and gate, while a copper fountain showers into a handsome stone basin.

Hidden among the flowers and camouflaged by a large earthenware jar is an ordinary pipe which serves to fill this pool.

For those months which have an "R" in them, one should be protected from the damp earth and above all from stone benches. Ideal are terraces and raised dry quarters where one can sit, play, or enjoy the sun without fear of catching chills. With infra red heating and an open fireplace, the terrace becomes a huge room without walls. An excellent location for such a nook is beneath a saddle roof, between sloping gable walls, or in a corner out of the wind.

Karel Capek recommends a terrace surrounded by a rock garden in which roof leeks and wall cress grow. But one should not be surprised, he says, if for the the first year the terrace looks as if it were surrounded by a refuse

TERRACES
AND SEATING ACCOMMODATION

heap. *The aubretia or rock cress which in the second year will cover the stones, will come as an even more welcome surprise.*

The best use of a garden terrace is open to discussion. Anything can happen there from gossip over coffee to a game of table tennis. The larger the terrace, of course, the more possibilities exist. This seems to be the only valid law.

Then there is the place of retirement — a small retreat where people can sit, somewhere among the bushes or against the wall of the house. There should be room for a hammock or a large sofa on which one can lie and do precisely nothing.

A cantilevered lattice sunshade provides shade
where needed and adds a delightful shadow
pattern of its own.

Sophisticated garden furniture brings indoor
comfort out to the garden.

This nook is ideally protected:
one side a wall with a painted scen
shaded by a Clematis-covered p
gola; on the other, by a house w
enhanced by a Wisteria vine; a
on a third, by tall flowering bush
and a Jacaranda tree.

An atrium or central court with a fountain permits private enjoyment of fresh air and sunshine.

An ultra modern garden room, open to the air, is shielded by a fibreglass sun screen and given great interest by the use of raised plant boxes, white pebbles, stepping stones, and a combination of sun and shade plants.

This arrangement for comfortable enjoyment of sun and shade and even gentle summer rain, adds a warm weather living room to a home. ▶

The terrace floor itself is the outstanding feature here with a checkered effect giving dimension and breadth to an odd-shaped area. ▼

Brightly printed cushions against the airy grace of white-painted wrought iron furniture.

This clever arrangement of flower boxes gives a sense of lush blooming while maintaining a feeling of lightness and order.

exotic canopy serves as a sun-de. The formal wrought iron fur-re is comfortably upholstered in catching print and colour to con-t rather than harmonize.

A new idea for saving space:
an awning attached directly to
the wall.   INVENTA

A well-designed summer
house provides shelter from
wind and bright sun, and
the convenience of a di-
ning area and a bar.

The inviting terrace of a Scandinavian country house makes good use of flowers in tubs and pots against a background of greenery and wooden fence.

Moulded fibreglass plant holders and laminated plastic table top are combined with hand-woven rush chair and stools to give a light-hearted, casual effect.

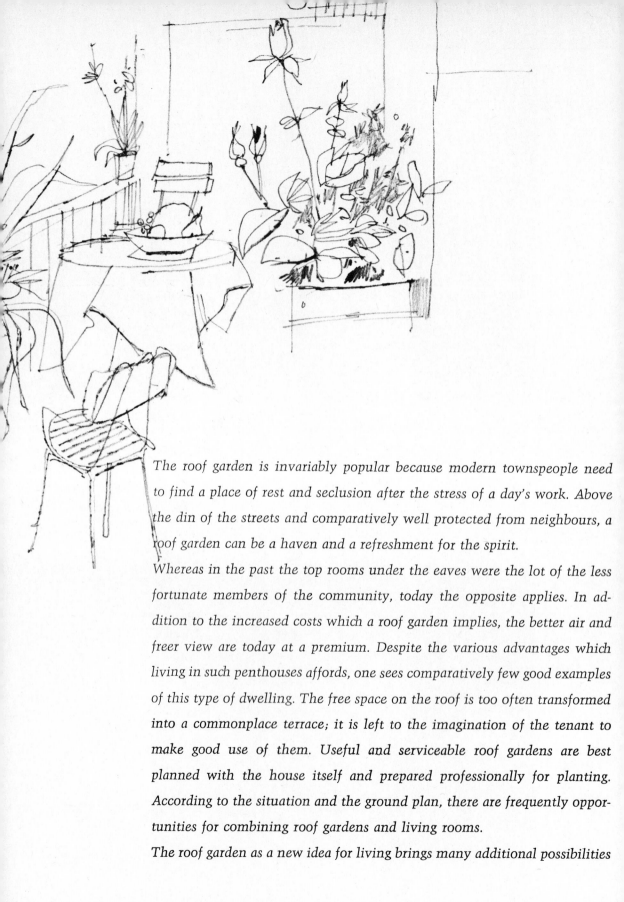

The roof garden is invariably popular because modern townspeople need to find a place of rest and seclusion after the stress of a day's work. Above the din of the streets and comparatively well protected from neighbours, a roof garden can be a haven and a refreshment for the spirit.

Whereas in the past the top rooms under the eaves were the lot of the less fortunate members of the community, today the opposite applies. In addition to the increased costs which a roof garden implies, the better air and freer view are today at a premium. Despite the various advantages which living in such penthouses affords, one sees comparatively few good examples of this type of dwelling. The free space on the roof is too often transformed into a commonplace terrace; it is left to the imagination of the tenant to make good use of them. Useful and serviceable roof gardens are best planned with the house itself and prepared professionally for planting. According to the situation and the ground plan, there are frequently opportunities for combining roof gardens and living rooms.

The roof garden as a new idea for living brings many additional possibilities *for a new way of life. The open living room, with the sky as a roof, brings a person back closer to nature. There is nothing more wonderful than to be awakened by the sun in the morning and, without having to get dressed, to be able to walk into the garden. One can enjoy, first-hand, a warm summer rain or a new snowfall. And on a warm summer evening, who would refuse an invitation to dine al fresco?*

Architect and landscape gardener should co-operate closely when making their plans. Many roof terraces, bare and lifeless, clearly show that the architecture is often impersonal and not designed as a human habitation. It remains for the landscape gardener to arrange his plants. For satisfactory growth, a reasonable climate and some protection are usually necessary. The architect should see that there are shady nooks, irrigation, and wind protection. The form of plant containers and the play of light and shadow afford the architect and the gardener plenty of scope to display artistic talents. Nor should the lighting be neglected.

While the architect creates the climatic prerequisites for the plants, the gardener must improve the residential climate for the tenant. Just as the minor details and the objets d'art give charm to a small room, so on a roof garden a wealth of flowers or beautifully shaped stones invite the visitor to observe and linger.

For the roof garden these are some of the possibilities: (a) An arrangement with inanimate objects. This has the great advantage of not having to be tended, and is therefore particularly suited to people who travel a lot and have no servants. A suggestion is an arrangement with stones, sand, water, withered trees and such. (b) An arrangement with living elements, with plants and living creatures such as birds, or fish in a pond, naturally requires

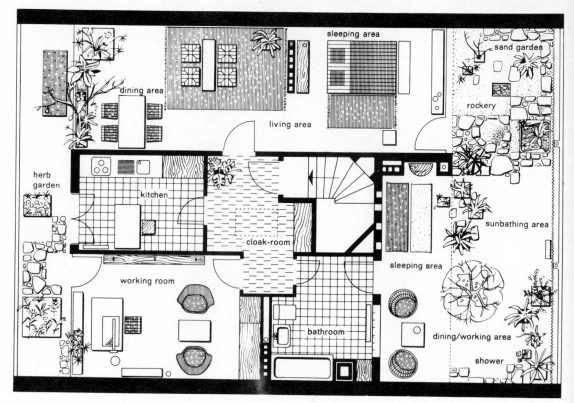

Suggested layout for a roof garden apartment

far more attention. This is quite simple with frequent use of a hose and other attentions, but when people want to leave in the summer, the immediate problem arises: who will look after the pets and flowers?

The heat that develops on a roof garden is so great that most plants start to wither after a few hours, and proper and frequent watering must be supplied. When tropical plants alone are used, a great deal of shade must be provided.

If the roof garden is to be used for various purposes, or if an ugly partition has to be disguised, moss or peat-filled woven wood boxes (or other containers) are excellent. These are made with a foundation of a trough-like lath or iron trestle covered with a wire netting. Subsoil under the wire netting will grow all the annuals usually grown in balcony flower boxes. Length and height can be according to the tenant's wish, while the breadth for a single-sided planting should be 8 to 10 inches. Once each week or two, the whole planter should be treated from above with a watersoluble fertilizer or a compost solution, until the water flows out at the bottom.

For the actual plant containers, excellent types are the large built-in concrete troughs which will give the plants enough room to grow for several years. If, however, one is confined to the use of commercial containers, products made of various materials are available. In addition to a suitable material, the shape is important. It should usually be simple and clear, without ornament or profile, its colours blending discreetly with the surroundings.

These specifications are excellently fulfilled by asbestos cement containers. The vessels are frost-proof and also have reasonably good insulating capacities against heat. One should be careful to use the largest possible containers, for in their case, the danger of drought and frost is far less than with the small ones. All plant containers should have holes in the bottom to let off the water, except those which are to be used for marsh and water plants or for hydroculture.

For obvious reasons, it is best not to let domestic pets run wild on a roof garden. Better suited are animals that live in water. In addition to pretty goldfish, the comic little water turtles which often go for walks outside the pool, and demand little attention, are to be recommended.

Tropical birds can be kept on roof gardens for the purpose of stressing the tropical or sub-tropical nature of the garden. Native birds such as blackbirds, larks and other small birds can be enticed by putting out containers in which they can bathe.

Since as a general rule the whole of the area is not intended as a roof garden, plan for hot and sunny, as well as cool and shady corners. Measures should definitely be taken for protection against the wind. By using architectural features properly, planting and satisfactory growth will be made easier.

In principle, one can use many of the plants found in the garden and even some of the smaller trees. Round the "lawns," bulbs, summer flowers, shrubs, and roses thrive as well as some evergreens, flowering bushes, and climbers. Rhododendrons, azaleas, and ivy are particularly suited to a northern aspect. The containers should be provided with a layer of gravel for drainage and filled with good garden soil. In moss containers, one can plant oak-leaved geraniums, petunias, ageratum, lobelia, and other annuals. Since the climate on a roof garden in mid-summer is very hot and dry, marsh and water plants and those that love dry heat can be recommended.

For marsh and water plants, vessels should be half-filled with loamy soil; this is preferable to the humus or richly fertilized soil which is used for the other plants. A number of greenhouses can supply reed-mace or cattail, water plantain, reeds, king cups and bog bean which can be found in many of our native pools. These varieties are content with a very shallow water level (about 8 inches) and do not have to be fertilized.

It is simplest to get the plants from a supplier and eventually to cultivate varieties such as the strikingly lovely dwarf water lilies available in many types. The care of marsh and water plants consists solely in giving them constant fresh water. In winter, the water can either be run off or led into a series of vessels.

There are often corners on the roof garden which are perpetually damp, and which receive comparatively little sunshine. There are plenty of plants suitable for these areas. Surprisingly easy to grow are china reeds up to

12 feet high, with silver grey whisks; they last well into the winter. As underplanting, laurel, wild violets, and various ferns are suitable.

For the walls or a pergola, the best-suited climbers are the many types of clematis and honeysuckle.

Among the annuals, sweet peas, convolvulus or bindweed, nasturtiums, and scarlet runners are effective.

Tropical plants often thrive on roof gardens. They are, with few exceptions, the smaller shrubs which are characteristically low-growing and do not, therefore, need such deep containers. House leeks, sedum, portulaca, and campanulas require little attention, and are content with little water. Among the taller plants the best are the various irises, evening primroses, and verbascum which like a great deal of heat and drought. Shrubs like tamarisk and sea-buckthorn make a good combination with ornamental grasses; they can safely withstand long periods of heat.

To assure a good water supply, the following advice may prove useful. The whole bottom of the container should be carefully laid with broken pieces of flower pot or other pottery, up to an inch or two high. Just below the surface of the shards, a hole should be drilled in the wall of the container, or in the case of a concrete trough, a tube inserted to allow for the overflow of water, and to see that the plants do not actually stand in the water. The water reservoir in the hollow spaces between the shards provides the upper layers of soil with invaluable moisture. Clay has the capacity to absorb water and protects the roots of the plants from growing in the water and rotting. How long such a water reserve will last naturally depends upon the outdoor temperature and the rain. The reserve must be checked regularly to obtain the successful results you want.

By J. Schnyder, Architect, and Gisella Schnyder, landscape gardener, Basle

This roof garden has been cleverly divided into lawn and terrace, with shade and sun both available.
MICHEL DE ST. PIERRE, PARIS

Heavy brown wooden beams give architectural dimension and contrast with the whitewashed walls. A pavement of fine gravel adds to the texture and spacious appearance.

other answer to the problem
privacy. Here a thick hedge
been planted around the
imeter of the garden.
LUCI LETERTRE, PARIS

A tiny pergola with a fast-growing Polygonum in a Japanese earthenware jar gives the illusion of a garden.

MME CRESSENT, PARIS

Evergreens, Ivy and shrubs have been used on this roof garden in Paris. The flower boxes are provided with gutters to catch the rain. The scarlet awning and the yellow and white tile floor are gay notes.

Trellises on the walls, a carefully tended lawn, and a well-trimmed hedge on a rooftop in Paris.

A lawn, a pergola, palm trees and tree Roses — a genuine garden high above the city roofs.

A highly individual roof garden. Cool ferns and water grasses grow about a shallow pool where one can see the antics of the fish and tortoises.

A charming contrast of yellow and
blue. Slipperwort, Petunias, Geraniums, and Daisies grow in flower
boxes and in jardinières along the
wall.

LANDSCAPE ARCHITECT: ALFRED REICH,
MUNICH/OBERMENZING

Elegance is the keynote of this impressive roof garden.

MICHEL DE ST. PIERRE, PARIS

ALEJO VIDAL QUADROS, PARIS

A particularly imaginative French garden arrangement. Tall reed matting covers the bare walls and gives a hold to the climbing plants.

Making the most of a tiny spot is this arrangement of white Petunias, red Geraniums, and small-scaled, light-weight furniture.

GARDEN ARCHITECT:
ATELIER "CHARLOTT", MUNICH

Flowers at the window can be a delightful vista, and a fine hiding place for a cat and its mistress to spy on birds, or to keep an eye on the neighbours. The box might be filled with geraniums which make an elegant thicket before the window, or a whole desert flora which lives behind the pane of glass protected, if possible, against the air in the room by a second pane. A little piece of tropical "jungle," too, can often be grown in flower windows. And what about an aquarium, by no means a rarity today? Many feel that a combination of both, with humming birds in the air, is better than all winter gardens, bird cages and aquaria put together. About 6 feet are sufficient to let a little brook flow into a lake. The water might be

WINDOW BOXES AND BALCONIES

18 inches deep behind the pane, and above the lush green of the tropical jungle, might hang sugar-water pipes from which the humming birds could suck the nectar, and lianas or vines covered with moss and orchids. The air above the water will be damp enough to allow these mysterious flowers to blossom behind the glass. (The smell might not be nearly so enchanting as the sight of these flowers.)

One can stare for hours into a flower window without growing tired. No cockchafers or beetles will ever be seen in them. There are pleasures which the city dweller can enjoy only if he has at least a balcony of his own where he can put the breakfast table for the family, and the necessary wrought-iron chairs.

But whether one has a window garden or raises cacti is a matter of personal taste. Certainly there are many other plants you may grow at the window which need little more than a watering can to keep them looking fresh and beautiful.

A concrete pergola on a city
roof is softened by climbing
Roses to make a glowing
frame for a view.

The balcony fence, laced with bright blue can-
vas, makes a fine background for the flower
boxes beneath.

Colourful flowerpots attached to shutters make spots of brightness.

Balcony window boxes crammed to overflowing with flowers, and a lavish growth of climbing Roses enrich this suburban house.

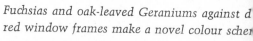

A pleasant arrangement of Nasturtiums, Daisies, and Geraniums enhanced by the yellow lacquer of the window box.

Fuchsias and oak-leaved Geraniums against d red window frames make a novel colour scher

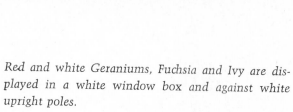

Red and white Geraniums, Fuchsia and Ivy are displayed in a white window box and against white upright poles.

188

The whole front of this house gains charm as the flower bed at ground level moves upward, visually, to the window sill and then to the balcony railing.

The facade of a house in Denmark combines
painted designs, window boxes full of blooms,
climbing vines, and a variety of ornaments such
as lanterns.

Hanging baskets are an additional way to display beautiful blooms on a balcony or roof garden, or even at a window.

From central heating to outdoor bathing in March is not so remote as it might seem. All one has to do is to lead the hot water into the swimming pool. A pump does all that is necessary and as a result, early Spring becomes more summery. It is a device that enables one to enjoy a little more fine weather. When the swimming pool is well-protected from the wind, and the sun is not too pale, little heat is lost. Thus a private swimming pool has advantages which for many people outweigh all the decorative attributes of a fountain.

SWIMMING POOLS

The question as to what a swimming pool should contain is answered very simply: fresh, inviting water. What it may contain may be something else — leaves from the surrounding trees blown by the wind into the water, for instance. Some owners of swimming pools have found it desirable to introduce a few carp or slippery trout. It is not unpleasant to bathe with the fishes. (Before a thunderstorm they leap for flies and are as attractive to the spectator as any sea lion!) Algae and water lilies, as depicted in the ponds of Gothic castles, are not to be recommended. Each to his own taste, but whatever means are used, the swimming pool should be kept clean and the water clear.

Glass mosaic lit from below, heating, fountains and cleaning apparatus will produce a dream swimming pool. The ideal size usually is about 18 x 45 feet. Some people enjoy the pleasures of bathing in a small basin dug in the clay and lined with modern plastic. It is stable enough to allow the children to sail little boats on a surface as calm as a millpond. Natural stepping stones or a flagstone path can give access to the pool.

Landscaping about the pool derives best from the individual setting and the characteristics of lawns and gardens around the house and grounds.

A Pompeian design with all modern conveniences.

This pool was created with the
house as part of the architectural
whole.

An attractive and informal arrangement of garden, swimming pool
and terrace.

A conventional rectangular pool surrounded by flower beds and ornamented with statuary.

The proximity of the sea and the southern sun make this pool seem an extension of nature. Mediterranean coast.

A beautifully balanced arrangement of colour:
the blue tiled swimming pool mirrors the sky
and the red awning is echoed in the floral motif
on the chair cushions, and in the flowers. A most
decorative and practical arrangement of the
outdoor fireplace, chimney, and woodpile has
also been made.

This graceful contour pool has been skilfully landscaped along its borders to blend into the scene.

The sun is captured here by a softly-toned bri
wall. The sky is mirrored in the pool and d
arrangement of potted shrubs, statuary, and la
terns and furniture make a serene retreat.

A large and unusually shaped swimming pool where the deep and shallow ends are separated by a small path. Spain.

Awnings, palms, white marble urns combine to create a near-Eastern atmosphere in this garden. A white marble pool is surrounded by emerald green lawn.

An elegant swimming pool with mosaic bottom and borders. England.

A beautiful contour pool set in red sandstone. Swiss Alps.

The colours of the canopied swing harmonize with coloured cement paving which surrounds this heated swimming pool. Stuttgart, Germany.

Listed here are those people and organizations who supplied photographs used in this book, and whose help we should like to acknowledge:

TH. ANDRESEN, FARUM
ERNST BAUMANN, BAD REICHENHALL
BAVARIA, GAUTING
CINE BRUNEL, LUGANO
CAMERA CLIX, NEW YORK
ALFRED CARLEBACH, LONDON
ALEXANDRE CHOURA, PARIS
GABRIELE CHRIST, STUTTGART
JOSÉ COMPTÉ, BARCELONA
STUDIO DESSECKER, STUTTGART
ERNST DEYHLE, ROTTENBURG
H. & B. DITTNER, BERLIN
RUDOLPH DODENHOFF, WORPWEDE
HEINZ GLEIXNER, MUNICH
HAGENBECK, HAMBURG
NELSON GROFFMAN, NORWOOD
HANS HINZ, BASLE
JOHN HARTLEY, LOS ANGELES
W. KORDES, SPARRIESHOOP
LAENDERPRESS, DÜSSELDORF
FRANZ LAZI, STUTTGART
HOLMES LEBEL, PARIS
SERGE LIDO, PARIS
ROTOGRAVURE, LEYDEN
MAISON ET JARDIN, PARIS
LEONORE MAU, HAMBURG
KARL MEYER, VIENNA
NICOLAS MULLER, MADRID
MUNGENAST + REUTLINGER, STUTTGART
ORGEL-KÖHNE, BERLIN
PHIL PALMER, SAN FRANCISCO
OTHMAR PFERSCHY, ISTANBUL
HEDDA REIDT, STUTTGART
SOCIETA SCALA, FLORENCE
SHINKENCHIKU-SHA, TOKYO
GENE STUTZ, ZURICH
ROSEN TANTAU, UETERSEN
KARL UND HELMA TOELLE, MUNICH
TRANSWORLD FEATURE SYNDICATE, LONDON
WALDVOGEL, ZOLLIKON